More *than a* Wheelchair

KENNETH POOLE

PAGE PUBLISHING, INC.
Conneaut Lake, PA

First originally published by Page Publishing 2020

ISBN 978-1-6624-2103-7 (pbk)
ISBN 978-1-6624-2104-4 (digital)

Printed in the United States of America

Introduction

Everyone has a disability. I may not be able to see yours, but it's impossible to miss mine. I'm in a wheelchair. It's easy for people to judge me by my wheelchair and not look any deeper into who I am. But the wheelchair doesn't tell my story, and people with disabilities often don't have a chance to tell their story. It's important that we talk about our disabilities in order to communicate what we're going through. Disabilities can make life hard enough, but when people are constantly looking at you weird, it gets even harder. I wish they knew a little about my story.

My name is Kenneth. One day I decided to sit down and write some of my feelings about my situation. I have a lot of feelings—if you used to walk and now you're in a wheelchair, you know what I'm talking about. This little book is about three people who ended up in wheelchairs. Richard, Kevin, and Q came from different backgrounds. Richard was a police officer that came from a good family. Kevin was shifted around with his brother and sister from foster home to foster home. Q grew up poor and his mom's family didn't want anything to do with his mom. We all have a Richard, Kevin, or Q in our lives. Their stories are unique, but what happened to them happens to people across the country every day. But they have something in common; they all ended up in a wheelchair in just a blink of an eye.

Richard

My NAME IS Richard, and this is my story. I never thought I would be in a wheelchair. I was born in a small town of Mississippi called Batesville. I was the only child, so I guess you could say I always got what I wanted. I was ten years old when we moved to Tennessee. My dad got a job at Vanderbilt as a professor. My mom was a stay-at-home mom. We lived in a very nice neighborhood, and I went to a very nice school.

Jumping ahead a couple of years, I married the love of my life, my high school sweetheart, Jamie. When I was in the ninth grade, as soon as she walked into the classroom, I knew she was going to be my wife. From then on, we were together. I asked her to marry me when we were in the twelfth grade. She said she would like to finish college first, so she went to Vanderbilt to be a doctor, and I went to Nashville Diesel College. We didn't see each other as much, but when we did, we always made the best of it. We used to stay on the phone until two o'clock or three o'clock in the morning. Sometimes I would fall asleep on the phone while talking to her! She was my best friend, and I could talk to her about anything.

I was doing badly in one of my classes and thought about dropping out. She encouraged me to stay in class; she didn't want me to give up. It made my life good to have someone like that in my corner that I could talk to about anything. I could not talk to my mom or dad about things like that. Don't get me wrong, I could talk to my mom and dad; but since I was the only kid and always got what I wanted, they would be like, "Okay, you can quit."

Fast forward to my second year in Diesel College. She was in her fourth year at Vanderbilt. I made up my mind to ask her to marry me again. I was going to do it right this time. I went in to talk to my mom and dad. I asked my mom, "How did Dad propose to you?" She said they had a barbecue on Father's Day and he asked her in front of the whole family.

Next, I went over to Jamie's house to talk with her dad. We had a long conversation about me and his daughter.

"I love your daughter so much," I said. "I will make her happy. I would like to ask for you and your wife's blessing to marry your daughter."

They said, "Yes, we would love to have you for our son-in-law."

I told them that I wanted my proposal to be perfect, something she'd never forget. I asked if they had any suggestions.

"No," he said, "it has to come from you, from the bottom of your heart."

The next day I called some people from her church, told them what I was planning, and asked if they could help me. Everyone said yes! That Sunday, after church, the whole choir stood outside the church. When she came out, they were singing "Differences" by Ginuwine: *My whole life has changed since you came in, I knew back then you were that special one.*

Right then I walked between the choir members and got down on one knee and asked her to marry me. She said yes! I picked her up and twirled her around, and everyone started clapping. The day we got married will be a day I will never forget. My whole family was there, coming all the way from Mississippi. Her family and friends were also there. I was standing up there in my blue-and-white tuxedo with my best man. She had on a long white-and-baby-blue dress. As she walked down the aisle, the music started playing "All My Life" by K-Ci and JoJo. Hearing that song and seeing her walk down to me, I started to cry and cry. I was crying so much that I had to put on some sunglasses.

After the wedding, I went into the bathroom and prayed, thanking God for my wife. As the years went on, she finished up college and got a job in the hospital. I got a job at UPS working on their trucks. Then we bought our first home. The next year she got pregnant. I could not believe it; I was so happy for my child. But God didn't prepare me for what was going to happen next. She had a miscarriage. *What did I do to deserve this?* We both thought our world had come to an end. It was hard for me to be strong; how could I be strong for her if I'm not strong for myself?

She went into a deep depression and stopped eating. The only thing she would do is lie in bed all day, crying. She stopped going to work. I didn't know what to say or what to do. One day, her mom came over and talked to her, and she started to come out of her depression. I asked, "What did she say to you?" She replied, "It's between a mother and a daughter." I was just glad to see her eating and starting to go back to work again. The next two years were beautiful. She got pregnant again. I really didn't want to go through this again, losing another baby. We did everything the doctor told us to do, eating right and going to all of our doctor's appointments.

We ended up having a baby girl. I named her after my great-great-grandmother, who was a full-blooded Cherokee and lived to be 102. Her name was Spirit. The nonphysical part of a person is the seat of emotions and character—the soul. That's why I named her Spirit. I was so nervous when she was born. After we brought her home, I used to sit up in her room and watch her sleep for the whole first month. I was so happy. It seemed like time went by so fast; before I knew it, she was already walking. She started going to the day care center and really liked it. Right about that time, I knew it would be the perfect time to talk to my wife about me joining the police academy.

"So why do you want to be a police officer?" she questioned.

"All my life I always wanted to be a police officer, and I'm not really happy doing what I'm doing now," I explained. "I only went to Diesel College to make you and my parents happy, but I am not happy."

"If that is what you really want to do, I'm not going to stand in your way. I will support you in any decisions you make."

I was so thankful. "Thank you, that's all I need to hear from you."

The next day, I went to sign up, but it took me about a year to be an official police officer. I loved it, but I saw some crazy stuff. On patrol one day, I got a call about a woman who left her kids at home all alone just to get some crack. The kids were two years old, the same age as my little girl. It hurt me so bad to see that. People do not realize that we put our life on the line every day. Don't get me wrong, there are some good cops and some bad cops. I have a family, and I know how it feels to lose someone you love. I pray every day that I can make it back home safely.

After about five years, I had seen and heard a lot. One Friday night, I got a bad feeling. Something told me not to go to work. Around midnight, a call came over the radio that a man was beating his wife, and I was the first officer there. I saw him in the middle of the street with no shirt on. I guess he was on something. He kept saying, "I'M NOT GOING BACK, I'M NOT GOING BACK!" while he waved his gun in the air.

That was the last thing that I remembered. I woke up and saw a bunch of lights. I thought, *where am I at?* I saw my wife and my mom. My wife was crying, and I knew something was wrong, but I didn't know what. My mom grabbed her and started hugging her and telling her it was going to be all right. A nurse came over telling them I needed to get my rest, but they could come back tomorrow. I was still like, "WHAT IS GOING ON!" I tried to move and get up, but I couldn't. I couldn't talk since I had tubes coming in my mouth.

For the next couple of days, I just lay in bed. Doctors and nurses came in and out of my room. I was thinking, *Where is my wife?* Some of my coworkers came in and brought me flowers and cards. We all just talked and had a good time. Then my wife came in with my little girl. The doctor was right behind her. He asked my friends if he could have a minute with me. When they left, he told me everything that happened. He told me they did everything they could, but I would never be able to walk again.

I was like, "What do you mean?"

My wife was like, "Calm down, calm down."

"For what? He's telling me I cannot walk and you are telling me to calm down. EVERYONE GET OUT OF HERE!"

She said, "Baby, it is going to be all right."

It is so funny how people can tell you to calm down and that it's going to be all right when they do not know how you feel. They always say, "I know how you feel." How do you know how I feel? You don't. I asked them to turn out all the lights in my room. I lay there for a couple of days, then one day my mom and dad came in to talk to me.

My dad said, "Son, you have a family at home. They love you. That little girl needs her father. You got to be strong for her."

"I know that, but how can I be strong for her when I can't be strong for myself? It hurts me when I think about it. I will not be able to walk her down the aisle when she gets married or push her in a swing. Thinking about all those things I can't do no more, I feel like my whole life has come down on me."

"You were trying to help someone, but that was your job, it comes with the job. You knew what you were getting into before you signed up. You knew all your life you wanted to be a police officer, to heal people."

"I'm tired of talking, I just need some rest. Can you leave me alone please?"

"Okay, we will leave, but there's someone out here. They would like to see you, okay?"

In came my wife.

"What are you doing here?"

"Why would you ask me something like that? I'm your wife. I have a right to be here. I love you, can't you see that? For better or worse. You are mad and you're taking it out on me. I haven't done nothing, so why are you treating me like this?"

"You need to be with someone who can take care of you and that's walking, not me, someone in a wheelchair. I don't need no one to take care of me. I can make my own money."

"I don't care about that. I love you for *you*. The wheelchair can't hold you back. The only person who can hold you back is you. And I'm going to be here whether you want me to or not. I have some good news to tell you. Some of your friends came and built you a wheelchair ramp for you to get in and out of the house."

"Well, you can just tell them to tear it down. I don't need no help. I don't need no one's help. I don't need no one feeling sorry for me."

"Nobody is feeling sorry for you. You're feeling sorry for yourself and taking it out on everyone. I did not do this to you, and I'm sorry it happened. Why are you pushing me away?"

Someone was knocking at the door.

"Who is it?"

"I'm the psychiatrist. Your doctor asked me to come and talk to you. Can I have a moment of your time? Could we please talk alone?"

I said yes and told my wife I would see her tomorrow.

"I would just like to ask you a few questions. How are you feeling?"

"How do you expect me to feel?"

"I know this is a hard time for you right now, but do you think about suicide and killing yourself?"

"Why is it every time somebody gets depressed, people automatically think they're thinking about suicide?"

"No, that ain't me, I'm sorry I have to ask you. These kinds of questions are to see where you are and how you're thinking. But I do have some good news. Would you like to go to Atlanta for a few months? They have good physical therapy there. We think it would be really good for you to go there. You will be able to come home on the weekends after two months."

"Okay, why there?"

"They have a good hospital rehab center. Look, you will not be able to walk again. This place will prepare you to learn how to deal with your disability and teach you how to take care of yourself."

I realized this was probably the best plan. "So when do I leave?"

"We are finishing up all the paperwork. You will be leaving Friday morning."

Friday morning came along and everyone packed up my stuff. My mom and dad were there and my wife showed up.

"So why are you here?"

"I'm your wife, I should be here. I'm coming with you for a couple of days."

"Who's watching my little girl?"

"She's going to stay with your mom and dad until I get back."

I did not want her to see me like this at the rehab hospital. "I really would like you to leave me. I cannot do nothing for you. You deserve someone that can walk."

She rolled her eyes. "You are leaving for six months, why are you doing this right now?"

"I don't want you to come with me."

She came anyway. We arrived in Atlanta and found the rehab center. They checked me in and put me in my room.

The next day, I started my rehab: how to get out of bed and go to the restroom, how to put on my clothes and what to do if I fell out of my wheelchair. How to get back in it and how to wash my own clothes. How to check my body for sores. I used to get mad a lot, especially when I would have an accident on myself, which seemed like every other day.

One day, a man came into my room to ask me how I was feeling. I said that I was feeling good. He asked me about suicide and if I blamed God for what happened to me.

"No, I do not. It was part of my job. I knew what I was getting into before I got the job."

He asked me if I would like to go home for Thanksgiving.

"No, I'd rather stay up here and be by myself."

He told my mom and my wife, and they came up with my little girl. I hadn't seen my little girl in about nine months. I was so happy to see her. But I did not want her to see me like this. When they came in, I was sitting in my wheelchair. Spirit saw me and started crying, and she did not even want me to touch her, so she ran from me. I felt so bad. My mom took my little girl back to the hotel and my wife stayed with me. I had been talking to the doctor about me having sex. He said I can take a shot or take a pill; I just need to ask the nurse and she would get it for me.

When my wife went to walk my mom and my little girl down to the car, I asked the nurse for the shot. She said it would take about twenty minutes before it would do anything. About that time my wife came back to the room. She came over and kissed me and told me how much she missed me. One thing led to another, and we made love that whole night. I started to feel like myself again. But it was hard for me because I could not do what I was able to do in the beginning. She got up that morning, kissed me, and went into the bathroom to wash her face. She said that she had to go to work the next morning, so she went and picked up my mom and my little girl from the hotel.

She said, "I will be back on Christmas. Would you like me to bring your daughter back with me?"

"I don't know."

"She got to get used to seeing you like this."

"Okay, you're right," I agreed.

When Christmas came, my wife and my little girl came back to see me. My little girl was scared and crying; but when I got out of my wheelchair, she got in and played in it, rolling around the room. I told my wife that I would be getting out in February.

"Yes, I know. What are you going to do when you come back home?"

"I talked to my chief at the police station and asked if I could come back to do some volunteer work, and he said yeah."

She was relieved. "I'm so glad you will have something to do when you come home."

"I cannot wait to sleep in my own bed. We have a lot to talk about. I do not want you to feel like you have to do everything for me. I want to be able to do stuff for myself."

"Okay, but it is going to be hard to see someone you love trying to do something and you may not be able to help them."

"How will I ever learn if someone is always there to help me do stuff? I need to do stuff on my own. That is the reason I came up here, to learn how to do stuff on my own. You are not always going to be there."

The next day, when I went to rehab, I asked the therapist, "How can I get some hand controls to drive?"

"You got to ask your insurance, and they will pay for you."

"Okay," I said. "Are we going to be driving today?"

"Yes, you need a little more work on your driving, and we got to practice getting in and out of bed. Are you doing your stretching? You need to keep on doing that because it will help you."

"Well, okay. I'm leaving tomorrow. I haven't been home in a whole year, and I'm going to feel like a stranger in my own house."

"Who's coming to get you?"

"My wife is coming."

"We have everything of yours packed up, so when your wife gets here, let someone know and we can help her take your bags to the car."

I heard a knock on my door, and I said to come on in. It was my dad.

"I thought my wife was coming to get me."

"She was, but she had something to do. She says she will see you at the house."

When I got home, the wheelchair ramp had a ribbon on it. When I went into the house, I didn't see anyone. Then everyone jumped up and screamed, "Welcome home!" and my little girl ran into my arms. I was thinking that no one cared, but to see all my family and friends and half of the police force there to welcome me home, I did not know how to feel. I didn't know that I had this many people who love and care about me. I realize now that a lot of people that get hurt and end up in wheelchairs do not have family or friends to help them. That's why a lot of them commit suicide and get depressed, because they feel like no one wants to be bothered. I'm so happy I have my family and friends. When everyone left, my wife and I sat up until four o'clock in the morning talking about how I made her feel and how bad I'd hurt her. She began to cry.

"I'm so sorry," I apologized, "But the one you love the most, sometimes that's the person you hurt. I thought you deserved better than me. I was looking like, 'What can I do for you and how can I take care of you being like this?' I know what I need to do, I need to get with a support group that I can talk to about being in a wheelchair. Monday, I will call around, looking for a place."

The hospital gave me a couple of places I could call. I called one of the places, and I went there. I sat for an hour, and I really liked the place. Everyone was talking about how they got hurt and how they are making it work for them. I did not say anything; I was just listening. I saw one guy who seemed like he was mad at the world. He sat a ways off by himself and did not talk to no one. I wheeled over to him and introduced myself.

"My name is Richard. What's your name?"

"My name is Kevin."

"How long have you been coming here?" I asked.

"This is my third time."

"Cool, do you like it?"

He responded, "It's okay."

I turned to go. "Well, I hope to see you again next Monday."

Kevin was pretty quiet. "You might, you might not."

When I went home, my wife wanted to hear all about it. I told her about Kevin. I said, "He seems like he's mad at the world." She said, "Maybe he is, so why don't you try to be his friend? Maybe he doesn't have no one." I thought she might be right.

Next Monday, when I went to group, I saw Kevin. I tried to start a conversation. "How was your week?"

"It was okay."

I tried to dig a little deeper. "I'm not trying to get in your business, but how did you get hurt?"

"I was working at the store, and I got shot."

"Wow, sorry to hear that."

He responded, "And what about you?"

"I was a police officer."

Another guy came over to us.

"What's up, Kevin?"

"What's up, Q?"

"Hey, how you doing? My name is Richard."

"Nice to meet you."

"So, Q, how did you end up in a wheelchair?"

"A drunk driver."

My name is Richard, and this is my life. You can see anyone can end up in an accident or a wheelchair. I got hurt on my job, Q got hurt by a drunk driver, and Kevin got hurt on his job. Anyone can get hurt at any time. So why look at us like we have a problem or look at us like we have a disease? We are human too.

Kevin

My name is Kevin. A little bit about me. I like to dress nice, and I love the ladies. I *really* love the ladies. But that is not how I ended up in a wheelchair. I know I cheated death a lot. I know in my heart I should have been gone. This is my story.

Growing up, there was me, my brother, and my sister. My mom was not around, so we spent most of our life at our aunt's house. My sister went to live with her dad, and it was just me and my brother and cousin. I was fourteen when my mom came to get us. She always treated me and my brother differently. I think that she loved him more than she loved me; it was just little things about how she treated me. I started searching for love in other places, talking to older women. I really should be dead right now from all the stuff I did. I remember one day, I was at the store, some boys came in that did not like me. They tried to fight with me in the store. A man put them out. There was an older woman in the store. I asked her if she could play like she was my mom to get me across the street. She said yes. When I got across the street, they could not catch me for nothing in the world, and they were on bikes! That is just one of the things I went through.

Growing up, it was even worse at the house. I used to feel like my mom did not want me there, so I tried so hard to be accepted by everyone around me, and that got me in a lot of trouble. I'm not going to say I was the perfect kid. I know I did some stuff to my mom and hurt my mom. Like the time I was missing for two days.

Some days they beat me up so bad they broke my nose. Once, a bunch of men came to my mom's house with guns, looking for me. Those are just some of the things I went through. I knew I should have been dead a long time ago, like the time I was messing with a married woman. The husband came home and caught me in there and chased me up the street, shooting at me. A lot of the stuff in my life I know I deserved, but some of the stuff, I did not deserve. I recall a time a girl invited me to come to the center and had some guys out there beat me up with guns. You look at me now and say you're surprised I'm not dead; I think the same thing.

You just don't know how many times I wish I was.

All my life, nothing's been going my way. One day, I did something I will never forget. A guy robbed me, and I shot up his mom's house, so her sons came looking for me. I had to move out of my mom's house, and I did not have any place to go, so I went to the mission. I stayed in the mission for a whole year. I got in a program they have, and I learned a lot. They helped me get a job and a place to stay. I was doing really well; I had my own place and a good job and was going back to school.

Someone told me my father worked right around the corner from me. I had only seen my father one time, and that was when I was ten years old. I headed to go see him. I was so happy to see him. It was like after all I had been through, everything was finally working out. We lived right around the corner from each other, so when I got off work, we drove home together. He took me to meet my grandmom, aunties, and cousins. I was so happy to meet my daddy's side of the family and to be able to hang around him. I felt like everything was going well in my life. I had two good jobs, my own place, and a nice car.

One day, I was out and I ran into someone I grew up with. It was my best friend, but I had not seen him in years. I thought he was my best friend. But you know, whenever you are doing something good, the devil always seems to put somebody back in your life to bring you back down. We talked about things we used to do. And we started hanging out again. I knew this was a bad thing, staying out all night, calling out from work, going to different clubs. I ended up getting fired from my job and losing my place, so I had to move in with family members. They helped me get a job at a store. They knew the owner. Everything was going good for the first month. I did not remember a lot about that night I got shot. The only thing I remembered was waking up in the hospital, but I did not remember anything else. It was like I closed my eyes, and a lot of white light was around me, and I was talking to my grandma. I knew she was dead, but it was like she was alive. I was thinking to myself, *Where am I, and how did I get here, and what happened to me?* I saw a lot of people standing around, talking, but I didn't understand what they were saying. It took about a week before I knew what happened. What did I do so wrong to make someone shoot me? I just didn't understand and still don't understand. My condition didn't really hit me until I couldn't feed myself and I was told I would never be able to walk again. This is when I broke down. At that time, I just lay on the hospital bed, not talking to anyone. The doctor came in one day and said I needed to go to physical therapy. I asked why, and he said it would help me out a lot.

"Would it help me walk again?" I questioned.

"No," he responded.

"So why am I going? I just want everyone to leave me alone."

The doctor shrugged. "You cannot lie here all day feeling sorry for yourself."

That made me mad. "What are you talking about? You don't know how I feel."

"You need to do this, it will help you when you go home."

So the people from physical therapy came and started stretching my legs.

"Why are you stretching my legs?" I asked. It was painful!

They told me that it is good to stretch my legs so that they don't go still. I learned how to get in and out of bed and how to get in and maneuver my wheelchair. Two months went by, and it was already time for me to go home. I was so scared; there was a lot of stuff I did not know. The first day home, I got stuck in the closet. I felt so helpless; it is so different at home than in the hospital. Sometimes I felt like I was not wanted there, and I was too much to deal with.

Like the time I used the bathroom on myself and someone had to come and change me. I know they didn't like doing that, and I felt ashamed. I felt like they did not want me there, and I was being a bother to them. I knew it was too hard to take care of me. I was getting so depressed. I did not want to be there. I could not do anything for myself, and I did not like having to depend on people to help me.

I was able to go out of town for rehab for six months. It helped me a lot. They showed me how to cook, how to take a shower, how to clean myself up, how to drive, and how to be able to take care of myself. They put me in a job program just in case I want to go back to work again so I will know how to live on my own. You would think everything was going good, but I was still dealing with some stuff. I was not happy with my condition, and I didn't want to live anymore. I paid a guy to go to the store for me and get some sleeping pills. I took twenty pills. Someone found me on the restroom floor. They called the ambulance and took me to the hospital. I had to drink some black chalk. I stayed in the hospital for two days, so when I got out, I had to see a psychiatrist. *Why was he talking to me?* I picked up a lamp and hit myself in the head with it. Blood went everywhere. I went back in the hospital to get my head stitched up. Then they sent me to a different hospital. This hospital is for people that are going through something and that are having a hard time dealing with depression. I was there for a month. I did not feel like going to group; I just stayed in bed or watched TV. I had a lot on my mind, I just did not want to be there.

When I got out, my brother got me a place in the Towers. The Towers is like an old folks' home. That did not help me out, not one bit. Here I am, twenty-two years old, living around a lot of old people. I felt like my family did that so no one would have to take care of me or be bothered with me. They barely came to see me. I just used to sit, looking out the window all day. I felt like I had not done anything with my life. No woman would talk to me. I just didn't want to be there. Every day, I woke up thinking of a way to kill myself. I kept asking myself, *Why has this happened to me? I work every day, then someone comes in and shoots me. What have I done to deserve this?* It was so hard out there for me, and I did not want to live like that.

Everywhere I went, people were looking at me. I was trying to talk to people about how I feel and the first thing they say is "I know how you feel." You do not know how I feel, so quit saying that! Did you get shot? No. Are you in a wheelchair? No. And I did nothing wrong but work at a job, so you do not know how I feel? A lot of times, I'd just sit and cry, asking God why this had to happen to me. But I didn't get an answer. A lot of people say things happen for a reason. That's easy to say if everything is going well in your life.

I never had anyone sit and really talk about my feelings to. That was hard for me, so I held all my feelings inside. I stayed mad at the world and kept thinking of new ways to kill myself. People were like, "You do not want to do that, and if you do, you will not go to heaven." This is not something you want to hear. I'm like, "I don't care. I'm already in Hell." So one day, I was sitting in the house, and I decided to burn myself up. I turned on the stove on high, and I put a pan on it. Then I put some grease on it, and when it got hot, I threw it on me. It burned my body up really bad, but the next day, I went to work like nothing was wrong. But I got real sick at work. They called 911 for someone to come and get me. When I got to the hospital, my fever was a hundred degrees and something. When they took my clothes off, they saw half of my body burned up.

The whole time I was at the hospital, all I could think about was how to end my life. I was so depressed. One day, lying on the hospital bed, I tried to hang myself, but the string broke. I thought, *What can I do next?* The next day, the nurse came and asked why I was so unhappy and why I kept doing this to myself. She said, "I have someone I would like you to meet," and it was another nurse. She called her down to my room, and we talked for a long time, past the time she got off. She would even come and see me on her days off and bring me stuff and talk to me on the phone. That made my hospital stay go by real fast. I said, "When I get out, are you still going to come around?" She said yes. The day I got out of the hospital, she was the one who took me home.

She would come over when she got off from work, and I would cook her dinner. But I ran her off just like I did to everyone who tried to get close to me, seeing stuff like this.

"Why are you with me? You deserve someone who's walking. I can't do anything for you!" I guess she got tired of hearing that, so once again I was all alone. I remember one night, I was sitting on my couch. I pulled my gun out, and it only had one bullet. I put the gun to my head and shot it, but it did not work. I didn't know why. I was so mad; I just went to bed. The next day my mom called me, and we talked for about thirty minutes. I had to get myself together; I just did not want my mom looking down on me and being disappointed with me. So the next Sunday, I called my cousin up and asked him if I could go to church with him. It was pretty cool. The next Sunday, I went by myself. It took me a year before I joined the church. I have learned a lot by going there. Don't get me wrong, I still get depressed because it is so hard when you feel like you are all alone.

Q

MY NAME IS Q.

People always say that if they had money, life would be better. I say life is what you make it, and I made it the hard way. When I ended up in a wheelchair, did it change me or make me worse? My name is Q, and this is my story.

I was fourteen years old with three sisters living in the projects. My sisters have the same daddy, but I did not. My mom was raped at fifteen; that's how she had me. My mom dropped out of school at seventeen just to take care of me. Her mom put her out, so she had nowhere to go and no one to turn to. The counselor at her school helped her get into the projects, and that's how she met my sisters' dad. He was always drinking and jumping on my mom. He would never do anything for me; he always called me a bastard.

I never understood why he didn't like me until now. One day he beat my mom so bad she was in the hospital for a week. That was the worst week of my life; it was like I got whooped every day. The social worker at the hospital said if she didn't leave, the government would take her kids away from her. So they helped my mom get a place and got her a job, cleaning up hotel rooms making $8.75 an hour. I had to come straight home from school to watch my sisters because my mom worked nights. It seemed like I grew up too fast helping my mom raise three sisters, getting them ready for school and cooking. A lot of times, I went to bed hungry to make sure my sisters ate.

I never could go outside and play with the other kids. A lot of times, I would hear my mom cry, and I blamed it on myself. If she did not have me, she would not have gone through this. She could have finished school. I made up my mind to make my mom proud of me and help her in any way that I could. I tried to keep the house clean and do jobs around the neighborhood to help with extra money. One day, when I was walking home from school, a man asked me to come do him a favor. He gave me something to take to a car across the street, so I did. He gave me $20. I put $10 in my sock and ran home to give my mom the other $10. I told her I found it.

The next day in school, I ate like a king. Every day when I walked home from school, I would see him; and he would ask me to do the same thing, then give me a $20 bill. I never knew his name, but this went on for about six months. My mom lost her job for missing too many days. My baby sister had asthma, and my mom used to have to take her to the doctor a lot. She did not want to get a new job and leave my sister, so she stayed home to take care of my little sister. I got tired of seeing my mom crying every night and not having enough money to take care of us.

I made up my mind about what I was going to do. I would dress every day like I was going to school, but I wouldn't go. I would run errands for the drug dealers in the neighborhood, then they would give me money. She used to ask me where the money came from, and I would always think of a lie. Then after a while, she just stopped asking. It made me feel good to help my mom with groceries and the bills and giving my mom money to get my sister's medicine. I would still go to school sometimes and the kids would make fun of me about my clothes. Then I just stopped going to school altogether.

I needed to be there for my mom. My mom needed me and my sisters needed me. I was the man of the house at fifteen years old. I tried to work a job, but I knew no one was hiring me because I was too young. So I went to one of the drug dealers I used to run errands for. I told him my problems about my mom and sisters and asked for a job. He said this life wasn't for me and that I needed to go back to school. I said that I had some money saved up and I would buy my own drugs, so I did. I got robbed a couple times before I got the hang of it. By the time I was sixteen, I was making at least $300 a day.

I took care of my mom and sisters and bought them whatever they wanted. I bought my mom a used car so she could take my sister to the doctor's office without waiting on the bus. When my sister started to get better, my mom wanted to go back to school and get her diploma. She took a class in the morning so she could be home at night. I started seeing this girl that I had been looking at for a long time, but she never noticed me. One day, I saw her in the store. I was clean that day, and I asked her out, but she said no. When she went to pay for her stuff, I said, "No, I got it," and I paid for it. She saw the money and said, "Yes, I will go out with you."

I had never been anywhere, so I didn't know where to go. I asked her where she wanted to go. She said she wanted to go bowling.

"That sounds fun! Would it be okay if I bring my sisters? They never been bowling before."

That Friday night, we all went bowling. It was a good time. I kept on falling, trying to bowl. They were laughing at me, and my sisters had a good time too. Then it was about time to go get something to eat, so I asked them where they wanted to go. Everyone said pizza. After we got through eating, we went home. I called her to see if she had a nice time. We stayed on the phone till about three o'clock in the morning talking.

That morning I got up and was getting ready to go, and there was a knock at the door. My mom said there was someone there to see me.

"Who is it?"

"Boy, get up and see for yourself!"

When I got to the door, it was Kim. "Hey, what's up? I was going to call you." I turned to introduce her to my mom. "Mom, this is Kim. This is my mom. This is who we went bowling with yesterday."

I stepped outside so we could talk. "So, what's up for today?" she asked.

"You tell me," I said. "I was just about to go to the mall and get me some shoes and some for my little sisters. Would you like to go with me?"

"Sure, are you going to buy me something? I'm just playing, but you take care of your little sisters, don't you?"

"Yes, I'm the man of the house."

"So where's your father?"

"I have no father. I don't want to talk about that. Are you ready to go?"

She pulled out her car keys.

I asked, "You have a car?"

"Yes, I been driving everywhere since I was fifteen."

"Why didn't you drive Friday when we went out?"

"Because you said you was going to take me and your sisters out!"

I laughed out loud. "You are right. Can I ask you a question? Do you think you can teach me how to drive? I never had a dad in my life to teach me and my mom is too busy."

"I could do that, when would you like to start?"

"Today, right now."

"Okay, let's go somewhere I can teach you."

I'm a fast learner, so it took her about two weeks to teach me how to drive.

"So now I can go get my driver's license."

She said, "No, it is not that easy. You have to take a test. I can help you with that if you like."

"Okay, cool, so let's go get the book and study for it."

It took about three weeks to learn that book. "So now, am I ready to go get my driving license?" She said yes, so the next day, my mom took off, and we drove down there together so I could get my test. We got there around nine o'clock in the morning, and we did not get out of there until around two in the afternoon, but I did pass my driving license test. Mom asked if I would like to drive home.

When I got home, all I wanted to do was sleep. I slept the rest of the day. The next morning, I got up early. I knew a guy who sold cars, so I went and asked him if he had a car for sale. He said he did, he had an old-school Chevy. He would let me get it for $2,000, but it needed some work. "Okay, cool, I'll have your money on Friday." It took longer than I expected. I knew I would need some money to get the car worked on, so it took me about a month to get all the money together. I went to see him, and I gave him $2,000, then I put the car in the shop. That was about another three months. I had to get the engine worked on, get it painted, and put some rims on it.

I just lay in bed, relaxing and thinking that this was the first time I had the house to myself. My mom and my sisters were not there. I heard a knock at the door. "Who is it?" No one answered, so I got up and went to the door and opened it. It was my sisters' daddy.

"Why are you here?" I asked. He tried to come in the house.

"AIN'T NOBODY HERE FOR YOU!" I screamed.

He smiled and answered innocently, "I came to see my girls."

"They're not here, so you need to move around."

About that time, my mom pulled up. "Q, what is going on?"

I felt confused. "Why is he here? Did you invite him over here? After he has done to you, you still talking to him?"

"Who do you think you're talking to like that? I'm your mom, and you remember that!"

"Okay, if he's gonna to be here, I'm not."

I went in my room to get some clothes. I was so mad that I did not realize I didn't have any money but a $100 bill. I spent all my money getting my car worked on. I called Kim to see what she was doing. She was out of town visiting her grandma. We talked for a while, and I told her what happened. She said I shouldn't talk to my mom like that.

"Talk to her like what? You don't know what you're talking about."

"I just know what you're telling me."

"I'm sorry, I'm just mad, and I'm taking my anger out on you."

"You're okay, I understand. When we get mad, we all say stuff we don't mean. So are you going back home?"

"No."

"Would you like to pray about it?"

"There you go with that. I'm out. I will call you later on."

I was homeless for about two days. I knew Memphis always had a dice game at his house every Friday. So I called him and asked him if I could come. "Yes, come on." By the next day around twelve o'clock, I made $3,000. I took $600 and got me a hotel room. I was on the block the whole weekend. When Monday came around, I made enough money to start looking for a place to live. By Thursday, I had myself a place and I was moving in on Friday. They say money talks; it does.

I did not need any furniture, just a bedroom and a TV. That was all I had. The only thing I could think about was getting money, so I hustled day and night. I just went home to sleep sometimes. I was doing really well, and I got my car out of the shop. I still hadn't talked to my mom, but my sisters would call me every day and talk to me and tell me what was going on. I would go back to see them once a week when my mom was not home. I missed my mom. We were always together. I couldn't believe that she let a man come between us, but I got to do what I got to do. I felt like I was out there by myself: no family, no one to love me. Did I bring this on myself? When you're out here on the streets, you cannot trust anyone. I observe everything. A lot of people say they're your friend, but they're just out to see what they can get from you. A real friend is going to be there through the good and the bad times. I had no friends, so I just called everyone my homeboy. At twenty-five years old, I was still on the streets getting money. I still hadn't talked to my mom in years, but I still kept in close contact with my sisters. They told me how things were going, and I took them out once a month. They said my mom was working at the hospital now, and she put their dad out two years ago.

"Why you just now telling me?"

"She said she did not want you to know."

"Okay, thanks for telling me."

That Friday, I went to the club with a couple of friends. I didn't drink nor dance; I just like the music. I was at the table drinking some cranberry juice and this young lady walked up to me and asked if she could sit down. "Yes, my name is Q. What's your name?"

"Star."

"I like it. That's a nice name."

"Thank you."

"So what brings you out on this Friday night?"

"I'm not far from here. I'm just here visiting my grandma and my cousin wanted to take me out."

"That's what's up. So where are you from?"

"ATL."

"How long are you going to be here?"

"I don't know. Probably the whole summer."

"Do you think I can call you and maybe we can go out sometime?"

"I cannot give you my number, but I can call you if that is okay."

I went home that night and really forgot all about her. It took about two weeks for me to see her again. I was in the mall on Saturday afternoon, and I heard someone call my name: "Q!" I looked around and didn't see anyone, and I heard my name called again: "Q!" I saw someone walking toward me. She said, "It's me, Star."

"Hey, what's up? How you been doing?"

"I'm good."

"So what brings you out here?"

"I'm just looking for a dress. My cousin is getting married."

"So what are you doing when you leave here?"

"I have no plans."

"Have you eaten yet?"

"No."

"Are you hungry?"

"A little bit."

"I know a great place to eat. Would you like to go?"

"Yes, that would be nice."

"You can just follow me."

"Okay."

We went to a Mexican restaurant. She said that she'd never been to a Mexican restaurant before. "I think you will like it," I told her. She asked if I spoke Mexican. "No," I laughed. "I just like to try different food sometimes." We sat there for two hours, talking. I learned a lot about her, and I noticed we had a lot in common. Having someone to talk to made me feel better because I was able to get some stuff off my chest.

But she did say I needed to talk to my mom or go see her because what if something happened, then what would I do? What if my mom died, how would I feel?

"You're right, I'm just not ready now. I feel like she turned against me for a man and that hurts me. Can we please talk about something else? So how long are you going to be here?"

"About another month."

"And then what?"

"I'm going to start college."

"What are you going to college for?"

"I'm taking up physical therapy. I like to help people."

"Okay, laugh out loud. Help me with this bill, you got jokes. So what do you have planned for the rest of the day?"

"Go home, take a long shower, and get ready for tonight. My cousins are taking me to a party."

"When can I see you again?"

"When would you like to?"

"Tonight at the party."

"Okay, I will call you."

"Okay, that will give me some time to do some run around and do some things."

At that time, my phone started ringing. Who was it? It just kept ringing and ringing.

"Hello, Q! This is J. I need to see you right away."

"Okay, I'm on my way." I turned back to Star. "I gotta make a run. I will see you tonight."

When I got to J's house, he was standing outside. He said that he just got robbed. "So what does that have to do with me and my money? You think this is a game? I told you not to play with my money! Every week it's something new. I'm going to show you what happens when you play with me and think I'm a joke."

I went to the trunk of my car and pulled out a baseball bat and started hitting him. It was just like I went crazy. When I got finished, I said, "Now go get my money and stop playing with me." When I got back in the car, I did not feel so good. I had never done nothing like that in my life. But I know people will take advantage of you and I'm not gonna have that. You cannot be free-hearted on the streets. I went home, cleaned myself up, took a shower, and was sitting on the couch watching TV. Star called around ten.

"What are you doing?"

"Nothing. Just lying here, relaxing."

"Would you like some company?"

"Sure, come on over."

"Would you like me to stop and get you anything?"

"I'm good, thanks for asking."

"Okay then, I'm on my way."

"Cool."

I got dressed and cleaned up the house a little bit. Then I heard, "I'm outside!"

"Come on in, the door is open. You got here fast. So you would you like anything to eat or drink?"

"No, thank you. I'm good."

"So how was the party?"

"Okay, I just wasn't feeling it. You have a nice place. I know your girlfriend fixed this up for you."

"I told you I do not have no girlfriend. I do not lie. Can't a man have a nice place?"

"Yeah, yeah, yeah."

"So what do you wanna do? Would you like to look at a movie?"

"That would be nice."

"Get on the couch, I will put in a movie."

After a while, she said, "You are falling asleep already."

"I'm tired. I had a long day."

"Would you like me to go get you some covers?"

"No, thank you, but could you wake me up at three o'clock?"

"Yes."

I found myself falling asleep. I woke up around four, then I woke her up.

"What time is it? Four o'clock? I asked you to wake me up at three o'clock!"

"I'm sorry, I fell asleep myself. I'm not going to stay up to wake you up at three o'clock. Can I make it up to you?"

"No, it is my fault. I cannot blame you, I was just so tired. I will call you later on today."

"Okay."

So I went back to sleep and woke up around 1:00 PM. My phone was going off; I had four missed calls. It was J telling me he had my money. I got up and got dressed and went to the spot. As I was driving up the street, something didn't feel right, so I kept going and parked down the street. I saw J talking to two men I never saw before. I knew he was going to set me up because of what I did to him. I got out of the car, got my gun, and ran down the alley to be on the back side of them. I called J and said I was coming down the street now. When he stepped out, I just started shooting at him. The two men took off running and I shot at them, too. I got one in the leg. When I ran back to my car, I was so nervous. I had never did anything like that before, but it was either them or me. I drove back to the house and turned on the news to see what they said. It was all over the news, but they didn't have any suspects. The police said it was a drug deal that went bad. I just knew someone had seen me, but no one said anything. Then Star called, asking me what I was doing. "Nothing," I said, "just sitting here." She asked me what was wrong, but I said I was good.

"Do you feel like having some company?"

"Not at this moment, but you can come later on."

"Okay, I will. Have you been in the house all day?"

"No, I went to the store."

"Have you been watching the news?"

"No, what happened?"

"It was a shooting. Someone got killed."

"Where at?"

"Out east."

"Wow, I haven't heard about that. So did they say anything else?"

"No, I don't know. I turned it off. So would you like me to bring you something to eat when I come?"

"Yes, did you cook?"

"My family cooks every Sunday."

"So how was church?"

"It was good. You should come one Sunday."

"Why? So they can look and stare at me and judge me? I'm good. I get that on the streets."

"You have good people and bad people wherever you go, so don't put that off on the church. Have you ever been to church?"

"No."

"So how do you know then?"

"I don't know, but I see how everyone dresses up to go. I thought you had to dress up."

"No, it is not like that. You can come just how you are."

"I might come one day, but right now, I'm just not feeling it. Are you going to bring me something to eat or we going to talk about church all day?"

"I'm on my way. Do you have something to drink or would you like me to stop and get something?"

"You can get me some juice."

"Okay."

I called my sisters. "How has everyone been doing?"

"Good, why haven't you been calling us?"

"I'm sorry, I've been so busy these last couple months."

"Mom asked if we've talked to you. I told her no. She's very worried about you."

"Tell her I'm good. So what's up? What have you been up to?"

"Nothing, just going to school. Why have you just stopped calling and coming by? I miss you. We all miss you."

"I'm sorry again, and I will try to do better. I love you, and let me call you back. Someone is at the door."

"Okay."

"Who is it?"

"It's me, Star."

"The door is open."

She came inside. "What are you doing in here? I thought you were going to put on some clothes."

"I just got off the phone with my sister. She was telling me they missed me, and they feel like I forgot all about them."

"Well, you know I'm going back home next week."

"No, I did not know that."

"College starts back next week and I have to go."

"So what are you telling me?"

"I just told you. I'm leaving next week, and I will try to come down here on the weekends. But the first couple of months I will be real busy."

"Wow."

"You knew I was going back to school when you got involved with me."

"Yes, I knew, but I did not think it was going to be this fast."

"So are you going to eat or not? Your food is getting cold."

"Yes, but you know what I really want to eat?"

We made love all night and the next day, too. I never felt this way about anyone before. I was twenty-five years old, and this was my first time. I did not know what to do or what to think.

"I have feelings for you, and I never feel this way about anyone beside my mom. You always here for me. I can talk to you about anything. You make sure I eat. No one ever cared much about me like you do."

"I do not know what to say. I did not know you felt like this."

"I do."

"So what are you going to be doing when I'm away at school?"

"Working, like I've been doing."

"Working where? You always have money, and I never see you working. Can I ask you a question? Do you sell drugs?"

"Why would you ask me that?"

"That is a yes or no question, and do not lie because I'm pretty sure I already know the answer."

"Yes, I do. I had to. I had to help mom take care of my sisters. I dropped out of school and started selling drugs."

"So are you going to at least try to get your GED?"

"Why? For what?"

"You cannot sell drugs all your life."

"This is all I know."

"No, it's not. Don't use that excuse. Would you want your sisters dating someone who sells drugs?"

"No."

"So you have to set an example for them."

"I know, but you do not know what we went through."

"You are not the only one that had a hard time growing up. My little brother got killed at twelve years old in a store robbery. He was just going in there to buy something to drink and got shot, so don't you tell me about hard times. I woke up today screaming just thinking about it."

"I'm so sorry to hear that. I know that this is no future, and I'm going to get out and do something better for my life."

"That's all I ask, you can come with me if you like."

"I wish I could. I have to be here for my family. I cannot leave my sisters and mom like that. But I will come every week."

It had been two weeks since Star left, and I felt like I lost my best friend. She called me every day, but it just wasn't the same. Weeks turned into months. Getting a call every day turned into getting a call once a week. So I said forget it, and I started back going out. I was in the mall, and I heard someone yelling my name. I looked around and didn't see anyone. I heard it again: "Q!" I looked up, and it was Kim.

"What's up, girl? I did not recognize you."

"What have you been doing, looking all good, boy?"

"Stop that!"

"I've been in school."

"Wow, you didn't tell nobody you was leaving."

"I'm back now and got my nursing degree."

"That's what's up. I'm proud of you. Where are you working at?"

"Vanderbilt. I been there for about six months now. Well, enough said about me. What have you been up to?"

"Same 'ole, same 'ole, in the street trying to get this money."

"So how are your mom and sisters doing?"

"Everybody's doing good. So what's up, are you seeing someone?"

"You can say that."

"So can we go out for drinks or dinner tonight?"

"Can he come?"

"Yes, he can come. I'll order him something off the dollar menu."

"Real funny, Q. So who is Star?"

"Wow, just a friend, but she's gone back to college."

"Well, just call me later on, Q."

When I got home, Star called me and told me she was pregnant.

"I haven't heard from you in months!"

"Once again, Q, you're making it all about you. And you told me you was going to come up here every weekend; you have been up here three times in the last nine months."

"Let's talk about that. And what have you been doing?"

"So you do not have manners to say 'You're right'?"

"I'm going to be there for my kid. My dad wasn't there for me and I promised myself I'm not going to do that to my kid. I want to be in my kid's life."

"Can you stop selling drugs and go back to school? Q, I am so scared that something is going to happen to you."

"Stop talking like that. Every time we talk you say the same thing: Go back to school and stop selling drugs. I'm good."

"Okay, well, if you want to be in your kid's life, you will have to change your lifestyle or you will not be able to be in his life. I'm not going to bring my kid up around that."

"Cool, I understand, but I had to do what I had to do at a young age to help take care of my sisters. But I'm older now, and I do not want this life for my kid. I wasn't going to tell you this, but since everything is coming out, I'm opening up a soul food restaurant next week called Star's Place."

"Why are you lying?"

"Have I ever lied to you?"

"No."

"I'm not going to start. Star, I love you and I want to marry you one day, you got to believe me. Can we talk about this later on? I have to go make some runs."

"Okay, be sure to call me when you get back home."

Wow, I thought. *A kid. I'm not ready for a kid right now.*

Star and I talked a few times that week, but pretty soon she completely stopped talking to me. I didn't talk to her for months. She said when I quit running the streets, we could talk. I wasn't ready for that yet.

One day I couldn't stop thinking about Star. I needed someone to talk to. I finally decided to give Kim a call.

"Kim, we still going out eat and get a drink?"

"Yes, meet me at the restaurant in twenty minutes."

"Okay, I'm on my way."

"What's up, Q?"

"Hi Kim!"

"What's wrong?"

"It's my girl, she is pregnant and I'm not ready for that."

"That's good news."

"I'm not ready for kids right now."

"Well, I guess you better get ready."

"I don't know what to do. Can we just take a rain check? I just don't feel like myself tonight. I have a lot on my mind."

"Okay, just call me if you need someone to talk to."

"Oh, I will do that. I will give you a call later on."

The last thing I remember was getting into my car. I woke up in the hospital with tubes in my mouth, and I remember my family standing around. I can remember my mom yelling to the nurse that I was awake. I was just thinking to myself, "What happened?" I found out I was in a coma for a month. I was hit by a drunk driver who ran a red light. The doctor talking to my family said that I would never walk again. I started crying. I heard a voice say, "What are you crying for?" I looked up, and it was Star holding a baby. "Whose baby is that?"

"That is your baby."

"What! Come over here and let me see. Wow! He looks just like me. What am I going to do now that I have a kid?"

"You can be there for him," Star replied softly.

I shook my head in disgust. "Why would you want to be with someone who is going to be in a wheelchair for the rest of his life? You deserve better."

Star smiled. "Right now, the only thing that matters is that we have a kid together."

"You sure do know how to make a person feel good."

Star asked, "Q, can I stay at your house till you get out?"

"Yes, my sister has the keys."

"Okay, I'm going to come up here tomorrow and ask your sister if she can come babysit."

"So what are you going to do about school?" I asked.

"Don't worry about that. You just get better."

"So what do your parents have to say?"

Star smiled again. "I love my parents, but I love you too, and I need to be here for you, and your son needs to know his father. With that being said, I will see you tomorrow."

At night, I would lie in my hospital bed, looking out the window, trying to figure out what I was going to do. I felt like everything came down on me at once. Six months went by real fast. The doctor came in my room and said that I would be able to go home the next day. It seemed like everyone was happy, except for me. The next morning, my mom and sisters came up to help me pack. Everyone was excited to take me home. The nurse helped me get into the car, and Star tried to break my wheelchair down. She tried and tried, but couldn't do it. The nurse finally had to help her. It was so funny that I laughed and laughed. That was the first time I had laughed in six months. When I got home, it felt so good to be in my own house.

But reality kicked in real quick. I just sat looking out the window for a long time. I did not feel like talking. I thought about my son lying on the bed, smiling at me. What am I going to do? I felt like I messed up my whole life. I knew I had to make a change. Six months later, Star was working and going to night school. She kept on telling me to go back and get my GED, so I went to sign up. My little sister babysat while I was at school and it felt strange being back in the classroom, but I knew I had to do it. Being in school helped keep my mind off being depressed and in a wheelchair. It kept me busy. But sometimes, late at night, I would lie in bed, wondering if God really does hear my prayers. I have done bad, but I also have done good. I guess it's true what they say, what goes around, comes around. I had been going to GED classes for five months, and I was finally ready to take my GED test. I took it the next week and they said it would take a week before they let me know the results. It seemed like I was waiting forever. It came in the mail a week later— passed! But I still was not happy. It was just a piece of paper to me, and I felt like I was missing something. What was a GED going to change? I'm still going to be in a wheelchair.

Star didn't agree. "No, Q, don't think like that. It is going to change a lot. You can get a job."

"Who is going to hire me? Look at me? What can I do?"

"You can do a lot. You thought you wouldn't be able to get your GED, but you did. You just need someone to talk to who has been in a wheelchair for a long time. They can help you. I'm going to call the city and see if they have someone or a class that you can go."

The next day she sent me to go meet some people in wheel-chairs that got together once a week. I really didn't want to go, but to make her happy, I went. It was okay. I learned a lot and met some okay people. I did not know there were so many people in wheel-chairs, and they had jobs.

When I got home, Star wanted to hear all about it.

"So are you going to keep going back?" she said.

"Yes," I replied. "It's something for me to do."

"Can I ask you a question?"

"What is that?"

"Can you please come to church with me, Sunday? I did not want to tell you, but I'm getting baptized, and I want you there."

"Wow! You know I've never been inside of a church. Why would you pop that on me at the last second? Everyone is going to be looking at me. I don't like that."

"Are you going to support me or are you worried about what people think about you?"

I rolled my eyes. "I'll go for you."

As she helped me in the car, Star remembered how difficult the wheelchair was to pack up. This was the first time we rode together since I came home from the hospital. "How do I do this again?"

"Okay, I'm going to jump in the car, and you push the button, and it takes my wheels off. Put them in the back seat. Put the wheelchair in the trunk. That's how you break down my wheelchair."

She pushed the button, pulled the wheels off, pulled the string in the back so the back of the wheelchair would come down, and put it all in the backseat and the trunk. "Wow! That was so easy."

When I rode inside the church, it was nice and the people were nice to me. I did not think it was going to be like that. When she got baptized, it was like I got baptized. He started preaching, and it was like he was just talking to me. It felt like I was the only person in there. I got to thinking about the things I used to do, and I started to feel bad. I was beginning to feel so bad that I started to cry. But I knew I had to hear more about this God he was talking about, so the next Sunday, I was up ready to go before she was. She was like, "Where are you going?"

"To church."

I was going to church every Sunday and going to Bible school class on Wednesdays. It took me a year before I joined the church. I still felt like I was missing something in my life. I didn't know what it was, so that Monday, I asked the support group. Everyone had something different to say, but I was just glad to have people to talk to that were just like me. Being in a wheelchair, it is hard, but if you have some good people to talk to, it makes your life easier. I heard a lot of stories about people committing suicide just because they were going through depression and didn't have anyone to talk to, or their wife had left them and they didn't have any family. I know that must have been hard for them. But my family was always there for me. I did get a little depressed sometimes, but knowing I had a son kept me strong in wanting to do better. The next year, I joined the church. Six months after that, Star and I got married. We had another kid, a baby girl. Do I still get depressed sometimes? Yes. But that is a part of life. I have a beautiful wife and two beautiful kids. Life moves on. I know I did a lot of wrong, but I cannot let it stop me from going on with my life. You got to realize that there will always be some people out there talking about your past and trying to break you down, but you got to look over that and try to find a good support group. Some people you can talk to.

About the Author

DESPITE DROPPING OUT of school and experiencing a lot of setbacks in life, Kenneth Poole seeks to inspire others through his story. He started writing this book five years ago. He never thought he would get this far. There have been times when he wanted to give up and throw the whole thing away. He just really wanted the world to see what he was going through and how he felt about certain things. He wanted this book to help anyone in any kind of way. If it has served its purpose, he is happy and content with that. This is from a guy who was told that he was not going to be anything, and he was not going to make it. His teacher said he would not make it to see twenty-one. But when he turned twenty-one, he went back to see her and said, "You lied, I did make it to twenty-one." The next week, he was shot at his workplace. He really hopes the book helps people because it has helped him to talk about what he has been through.

CPSIA information can be obtained
at www.ICGtesting.com
Printed in the USA
JSHW040501080621
15659JS00001B/51

9 781662 421037